B. R. Duval

A Narrative of Life and Travels in Mexico and British

Honduras

B. R. Duval

A Narrative of Life and Travels in Mexico and British Honduras

ISBN/EAN: 9783337210694

Printed in Europe, USA, Canada, Australia, Japan

Cover: Foto ©Andreas Hilbeck / pixelio.de

More available books at **www.hansebooks.com**

A NARRATIVE

LIFE AND TRAVELS

IN

MEXICO AND BRITISH HONDURAS.

BY REV. B. R. DUVAL,
Late of the Virginia Annual Conference.

Present Address—Dispatch, New Kent County, Va.

THIRD EDITION.

—————

BOSTON:
W. F. BROWN & COMPANY, PRINTERS,
No. 213 Franklin Street.

PREFACE.

It has frequently been suggested to me that I ought to write an account of my trip to the countries from which I have just returned, as a means of making something for the support of my family, as well as affording useful information concerning those beautiful lands; and I now undertake to comply with those suggestions.

But, as I can spare very little time, I shall simply aim to relate such things as I would tell in a social circle, and in the same style; hoping that some good may be done, as the readers shall see the great religious privileges they enjoy, compared with the people of

Mexico, and their consequent obligations to God for a free Bible in our native tongue.

I am sorry that my want of means causes the price to be higher than it otherwise would be.

B. R. DUVAL.

BALTIMORE, *April*, 1879.

A NARRATIVE

OF

LIFE AND TRAVELS

MEXICO AND BRITISH HONDURAS.

—•-•-•—

On the first of December, 1864, I was living about twenty miles south of Petersburg, Virginia, near Stony Creek Depot, sawing lumber and grinding corn, at a large steam mill ; but before night nearly everything I had was stolen, or burned up, and in a few hours I was reduced from a comfortable independence to real destitution. But I did not repine, but exerted myself to the utmost, to support my family and pay my debts; and soon after the Surrender, I went to work and fixed up the saw mill, and hoped that at current rates, I might yet be able to saw lumber enough to pay out. But lumber soon fell to a price not sufficient to pay expenses; and as soon as I saw this, I went to a most honorable lawyer, and asked him to make a deed of the most equitable character, and sell ▓▓▓▓▓▓ for the benefit of my creditors. This was done, and we received only the allowance made by law to insolvent debtors.

This was in May, 1866, and I was at a loss to know what to do. I could hear of no place where I could be supported, as a preacher, and my presiding elder told me that he knew not what to advise, as the times were such that he hardly knew how to advise himself.

About this time, I had seen accounts in the papers of a settlement of Southern people in Mexico, under the auspices of such men as Captain Maury, General Price, and others of high character; and these accounts stated that the whole number amounted to 5,000. From one of these publications I inferred that there was no *Methodist* preacher among them, and I felt that there was the place for me, if I could get there; and it certainly seemed providential, when I found a friend who would advance me the necessary amount. My deliberate judgment, formed after much earnest prayer and the cheerful concurrence of my family, then was, that it was my *duty* to go to Mexico, and my hope was that I could support my family by working as a surveyor, for which I had prepared myself, and preach gratuitously to my countrymen till I could organize a church.

Accordingly, on the 22nd day of May, I started from Petersburg, with Mrs. Duval and three daughters and a son, for New York, to take passage by steamer Manhattan, for Vera Cruz, by Havana.

The weather was very pleasant, and soon after getting in the Gulf stream, we saw a beautiful phenomenon, of which I had never heard. It was late in the afternoon, and the atmosphere was misty, and there appeared over a great part of the sky hundreds of rings just the size of the sun, very bright, and clearly defined. The sight was very novel and beautiful, and the surgeon of the ship told us that he had only seen it a few times, and then only in the Gulf stream.

I was very much pleased to see the children so much interested in looking at the flying fish, the nautilus, the beautiful dolphins, with their colors changing like chameleon, the sea birds, and other things seen only on the ocean.

There were several very agreeable travelers on board, and one of them was especially kind to us. He was a Spaniard, who had a large wholesale house in New York, and was going to Havana. Having heard our history, he feared that we should have hard times in Mexico, and having seen that we had four children, corresponding in age and sex with his four children, that he was in great

comfort at his country seat near New York, he showed
our children the four buttons on his wristbands
which contained the likenesses of his children, and
wept bitterly, saying, that he felt very much for us
After awhile he told me that before he reached Ha
vana he would give me a letter to a friend in Vera
Cruz, which he *knew* would do me good. And indeed
it did, for it contained an order for fifty dollars in
gold. As he was about to leave the ship, in Havana
he shook hands with me and Mrs. Duval, most cor-
dially, and kissed all the children, as affectionately
as if they were his own, and was too much affected
to speak.

This kind-hearted man, and several others of his
nation, have satisfied me that there are many who
are not protestants whose actions look more like the
Christianity of the New Testament than the actions
of many who boast of their evangelical faith.

The time of our stay in the beautiful harbor of
Havana was too short to give us a chance to see
much of this famous city, but the church in which
the remains of Columbus are deposited was pointed
out to us, and awakened peculiar thoughts in our
minds What wonderful results have followed from
the enterprise of that great man ! And how different
would have been the history of the world, if Columbus
had di   land twenty degrees further north.

9

We reached Vera Cruz at night, after a passage
of four days from Havana, and anchored near the
famous castle of San Juan D'Ulloa. Next morning
we entered the renowned city of Vera Cruz, a walled
city of about 10,000 inhabitants. We were struck
with the great politeness of the people of all classes,
and especially of the officers of the custom house.
Arrangements had been made by the government
for the encouragement of persons coming into
Mexico to settle, and our railroad fare was only
one-fourth of the usual rates.

The weather was extremely hot, and the yellow fever had just commenced its annual work, and we hur-
ried up the country next morning on the imperial railway. This great railway is the work of an English
company, and is intended to connect the city of
Mexico with Vera Cruz, about two hundred and
fifty miles off, but was only complete forty-seven
miles to the first mountains, and has a very good
grade, over ground at first low and swampy, then
sandy and somewhat rocky, but all very barren.

One coach was filled with Nubian soldiers, with
their rifles, and a small brass howitzer on each side,
fixed on a pivot at a window. These are very good
soldiers, of warlike Mahometan tribes, of upper
Egypt, and have been famous in Napoleon's wars
in the Crimea, and in Lombardy. They are very

black, but very tall, and very different in appearance and character from the African race in the Southern States.   They always attend the trains, especially to guard great quantities of silver, sent down from the city of Mexico to Vera Cruz, on the way to Europe.

In about three hours, we reached the terminus of the railroad, and took an ambulance for Cordova, where we arrived before night.   We were then 75 miles from the coast, and in full view of the peaks of Orizaba, which is 17,400 feet above the level of the sea, and is always covered with snow, to the amount of about 500 acres, cooling the air, very perceptibly, for fifteen miles around.

On the Sunday after reaching Cordova, I called on the alcade, or mayor, and told him that I wished to preach that afternoon at the Confederate hotel, according to invitation.   He said, "Very well, you have perfect liberty, according to the decree of the Emperor Maximilian."   I told him that I was aware of that, but that I wished to pay my respects to him, and let him know my purpose.   Accordingly I preached at the appointed hour, and kept it up during the three months that we lived in Cordova. However, none but Americans attended, as the mass of the people are Roman Catholics.

At this time, there was great anxiety in Cordova, on account of about thirty Americans who had settled below General Price's colony, and had been captured and carried off prisoners by a band of Liberals, as they were called, and who were opposed to Maximilian. The Liberals made heavy charges against the Americans, and, no doubt, some of the Americans were guilty; but after a few weeks nearly all the Americans returned, having escaped or been released; and then they tried to get Maximilian to indemnify them for all their losses; and having failed in this, they commenced trying to get back to the States.

'The approach of the rainy season, together with the uncertainty of Maximilian's continuance in power, caused the work on the railroad to be suspended, and I could find nothing to do, till I got a small wagon and a pair of mules for a piano which had been given one of our daughters, and which she wished to sell.

With this wagon I hauled freight from the Depot to Cordova, 25 miles, and to Orizaba, 40 miles, and thus I made out for awhile, till the roads became so bad that the mules got stuck in the mud, so that I had to pay $1.50 to be hauled out of a mudhole, and after going about 100 yards, I stuck again, and had to pay $2.00 more.

It was then getting very sickly at Cordova, while it was very healthy in Orizaba, and we removed to Orizaba, which is a very beautiful place of about 20,000 inhabitants. Here we were very pleasantly situated, the climate being delightful, and cool enough for a blanket every night. The market was very well supplied with meats and vegetables, at fair prices. The onions were the finest I have ever seen. Green corn could be had a great part of the year, and the quantity and variety of vegetables were very great. But the fruits exceeded the vegetables. Oranges were very abundant and delicious, and I could get choice ones for 12½ cents a hundred. Pineapples also were very abundant, and at Cordova I bought choice ones for two cents each, and sometimes one cent each, perfectly ripe and delicious. The fruits were too numerous for me to learn all their names.

But at Orizaba, as at Cordova, I could find but little to do, and we had hard work to live. I got some hauling to do, but not enough to feed us.

One morning, Mrs. Duval told me that we had nothing to eat, and no money, and asked what we should do. I said that I did not know, but that there was time enough yet for the ravens to come before breakfast, and that I would do all I could and trust Providence, as we had done so often

before. I then took my case of surveying instru
ments, and started out to find a Texan, who could
talk Spanish better than I could, to get him to pawn
the instruments for some money. I went into the
street, and turned up, and less than thirty steps, I
met my Texan friend, and asked him if he could
raise me some money on the case of instruments;
and he said "yes." I asked him when; and he
said "some time to-day." "But," said I, "we have
no breakfast. and I need money *now*. Can't you
lend me a dollar?" "Yes," says he, handing me
out two half dollars. I turned immediately round
and went home. On meeting my wife at the
kitchen door, I said, "Agnes, the ravens have come
already;" and having called two of the children, I
sent one for beef, and the other for bread, and in
due time we had a good breakfast.

In one of my trips, I went over the great mountains that enclose the high table lands of Puebla,
and it took about half a day to reach the top of the
ridge, where the road crosses. The elevation was
about 9 or 10,000 feet, and the climate very cool,
requiring two or three blankets at night. After
descending a little, I came to a great valley, inter-
sected at right angles by another large valley, and
near the intersection were the buildings of a
great estate, employing about 36 laboring men

Indian corn was the principal crop, and I think I saw more corn at one view, than I have ever seen elsewhere.

This corn was very good indeed, and I should think, from a view that I had of the field, from the side of the mountain, that the corn field in the long valley must have been seven or eight miles long, and nearly two miles wide, besides the short valley, which was richer land, and, I should think, contained at least 1,000 acres. What can be done with all this corn, one may ask.

The toll-gate keepers at Orizaba report that, on an average, 800 mules pass every day in the year. The corn raised on the great estate of Esperanza, can only furnish a small part of the amount required for these mules, and it is the lowest down the road of all the great corn plantations. The manager told me that he paid the 300 Indians 37½ cents a day for each day's work, and that with this money they had to buy food, clothing and everthing for themselves and their families. I supposed the profits on sales to the Indians must be 100 per cent., and then I should call the labor cheap.

In this valley I saw the plant called *maguey*, from which the Mexican drink called *pulque* is made. The plants are about six feet apart, and when about for years old, a flowering stalk begins to shoot up, and soon after it gets above the leaves, which are eight or nine feet high, it is cut out about one foot above the ground, and a large round hole containing about two gallons is scooped out and becomes filled twice a day with a thick, milky fluid, that oozes from the enormous leaves. Barrels are placed at proper intervals, to be filled with the juice thus obtained. At first the *pulque* is sweet, but soon ferments like cider, and makes a very nutritious and pleasant drink, but if allowed to ferment too much it becomes intoxicating ; and vast quantities of it are distilled into rum, greatly to the injury of the Indians, who are very fond of strong drink..

The plant, while furnishing the *pulque*, is dying all the time, and in five or six months dies and soon decays, and other plants then come on so as to keep up the supply. The leaves of a large plant are about fifteen inches wide, and seven or eight inches thick at the ground. and taper in width and thickness to a point, which is a very stout and very sharp spike, that is greatly dreaded by cattle, and this instinctive dread leads to the use of this plant for fencing. Two rows of the *maguey* plant are set out five or six feet apart, and when they are only one foot high, the cattle dread them too much to pass over them.

At an elevation of five thousand feet these planta will grow, but they will not come to such maturity as to make *pulque* until you reach an elevation of six or seven thousand feet. On the mountains nine or ten thousand feet high, they grow spontaneously, but are unproductive.

The *pulque* is much relished in Orizaba, and is brought on the backs of mules, in goat skins, and sold like cider.

The vast amount of hauling done on the backs of animals in Mexico, is a remarkable feature of the country.

Pack saddles are fastened on the mules, very securely, and such large mules as the regular muleteers use are loaded with four hundred pounds each, two hundred pounds on each side. The bales of cotton sent up from Vera Cruz weigh two hundred pounds each, and one bale is put on each side of the mule. Four boxes of wine or brandy, one dozen to the box, are also put on each side of a mule for a load, and other things in proportion.

I have seen, many a time, one hundred or more of these mules in a drove, led by a mare, partly white and partly black or red, with or without her colt. About two o'clock the drove stops for the day, and the mare takes her place at the end of the line, as directed by the drivers. The mules all form

in line, as soldiers, and the packs are taken off and
put just opposite the mules, and then the saddles,
and now when all the mules are stripped, a pop of
the driver's whip gives the signal to the mare and
she trots into the river or creek, and while they are
drinking a long cloth is stretched out for a trough,
and supported by forks and long ropes, with their
ends pinned to the ground by stout iron pins, and
this trough is then filled with cut-up wheat or barley
straw and corn poured all over it   When the mules
have done drinking, the driver's whip ₁ ops the signal to the mare and she leads the mules to dinner.
Two hours before day the mules are fed again, and
at daybreak they are led to water, and then to their
places in line, each one opposite his own pack.   If
any one has been careless and taken the wrong place,
the driver's whip reminds him of his error, and he
hastens to his proper position.   They are then
saddled and loaded, and the mare, with her little
tinkling bell, leads the way.

If a contractor engages to do a certain job of
masonry, he employs the owner of a drove of donkeys to haul the stone, the sand, and the water, and
all are hauled on the backs of the donkeys, and in
many cases it is better than to haul in ox-carts or
wagons, for the mountains where the lime and stone
are found are too steep and rock   ons, and

the banks of the rivers or creeks are also too steep for any sort of vehicles.

And even planks are hauled from the mountains on the backs of mules, one end being secured to the pack saddles and the other dragging on the ground. Large timbers cut and hewn in the mountains are dragged down by oxen.

The great wagon trains, that haul heavy machinery, have twenty-two mules each to a wagon, and a very large washer is put on each end of each front axle. A very strong hook is attached to each washer, and when the twenty-two mules cannot pull the wagon, a string of twenty mules from the second wagon is attached to one axle; and if the forty two mules cannot pull the wagon, another string of twenty mules (four abreast, as all are,) is attached; and if they are not enough, more are attached, until, sometimes, 122 mules are pulling at one wagon.

I have seen sixty-two, myself, but as they succeeded, the other sixty were not attached through the train consisted of twenty-five wagons, of twenty-two mules each. The mules are always four abreast, except the trains that carry silver, in which they are always two abreast, and twelve to each wagon. 'I have seen thirty-six of these specie wagons in front of my d   twelve mules to each, and all loaded with nothing but Mexican dollars; and escorted by a strong body of French soldiers.

These French soldiers were quartered near us, in both Cordova and Orizaba, and we saw a good deal of them on the road, having met them frequently; and we heard our countrymen, who had known them for years, speak of them, and from all I have seen and heard, I regard them as very superior troops. In camp they were very quiet and well behaved, and we were pleased to have them near us; and their politeness to us, on meeting them in the road, was remarkable, the highest officers saluting a poor American in his wagon, as if he were an officer of distinction. And their courage in battle was really marvellous.

At the fort that overlooks the city of Orizaba, a captain greatly distinguishe 1 himself by scaling the mountain side, where scarcely a goat could climb, and capturing the fort, full of Mexicans, and routing a whole army of reserves of about 2,000 men.

Another captain, holding a station on the railroad, about thirty miles from Vera Cruz, fought from sunrise to sunset, till his ammunition was exhausted and he and every one of his men were killed. The drummer, an Italian, recovered from his seventeen wounds, but all the six Frenchmen were left dead on the field.

without any sort of protection. The Mexicans lost about 400 out of their 3,500 cavalry.

As the train stopped I got out and looked at the graves where they are all buried together, which was surrounded by an iron railing and marked by a wooden cross, inscribed with date, names of officers and number of men who fell in this remarkable engagement. This inscription I read, but did not have time to copy.

The next day these Mexicans attacked the next station, ten miles off, and were repulsed by a company of Nubian Zouaves, who were ready to fight to the last, as their comrades had done.

While I was in Mexico, the Imperialists and Liberals had a fight near Matamoras, and an American who was in the battle told me that as soon as the Imperialists were attacked they went over to the Liberals, or surrendered, except the French, who consisted of one company, and they cut their way out, and the Liberals thought it prudent to let them go in peace—and I think that was a wise conclusion.

But now General Castelneau, Napoleon's envoy, came to see Maximilian and Marshal Bazaine, the commander of the French troops, and we soon learned that the French troops would return to France; and when I saw them going through Orizaba, to Vera I began to think that the reign of

Maximilian was very near its end; and when he himself arrived, on his way to Europe, as we heard, we could doubt no more. I saw him riding out daily for a week or two, and thought he would get off before we could; but as all our countrymen were preparing to go away, and our principal friends, particularly General Hindman and his family, urged us to hasten away, and gave all the help they could afford, we started off also.

We stopped in Cordova the first night, and saw General Price and family, and we felt very sorry to leave such noble and kind-hearted friends.

The next morning we left Cordova before day, and a little before sunrise we looked back and saw the snow on the summit of Mount Orizaba as deep crimson as the clouds in the east. As the sun rose the color of the snow faded, just as the clouds faded, till the snow assumed its usual dazzling whiteness. It was a grand sight. Five hundred acres of crimson snow more than three miles high!

Soon after breakfast we came to Mr. Fink's coffee plantation, of one hundred acres. I learned from him that the annual yield of coffee is from one thousand to twelve hundred pounds an acre, and that at the lowest estimate, allowing three cents a pound for expense of cultivation, packing, husking, &c. and thirteen cents a pound for the price at his door, there is a clear profit of ten cent a pound, or one hundred dollars an acre.

The coffee berry is very much like the black-heart cherry, but with scarcely any stem, each berry containing two grains. The berries are planted whole, in ground well worked up, and a scaffold about three feet high is made over the bed, and covered with large leaves, so as to protect the young plants from the sun until they are two to three feet high, when they are set out in rows eight feet one way and nine the other, and kept free from bushes, weeds, &c., until they are three or four feet high. They are then cut down with a sharp knife, about six inches from the ground, and four to five sprouts spring up around the little stumps, and are allowed to grow about five feet high, when the tops are cut off to keep the trees from growing too high.

The next spring these beautiful bushes will be covered with very fragrant white flowers that perfume the whole atmosphere, and these are soon followed by green berries, that soon become pink, and then deep purple, and then they are ready for gathering. They are then dried in the sun, daily, until dry enough to put away without danger of moulding, and in the following March, when the weather is hot and dry, they are dried throug in a trough until the grains are separated from the husk, and after being win-nowed and picked over, they are ready for market. This is the Mexican way of preparing the coffee berries.

The Brazilian way is said to be quite different. There they strip off the berries from the twigs, the unripe as well as the ripe, and soak and work them up in water until the pulp is washed from the grains, and then the grains are dried till ready for the bags,

In some places where the heat is very great, the woods are trimmed out, so as to leave only enough trees to shade the coffee bushes, and the coffee plants are set out so as to have the benefit of the shade. This was the case with Mr. Fink's plantation. In other places, suitable trees for shade are planted among the coffee bushes, while in other places, where the heat is less, the coffee needs no shade.

A coffee plantation will bear a full crop in four years from the setting out of the scions, and will last twenty or thirty years. I heard an old gentle-man say that he knew one, in southern Mexico, that is forty years old.

The chocolate beans are raised from trees, planted in the shade, like the coffee trees; and the profit of raising them is said to be greater; and well made chocolate is justly considered a great luxury.

About five miles before we reached the railroad
an axle of our wagon broke, and we had to ask help
of some French troops, who took my family in their
wagons, and, with the utmost kindness and politeness, carried them to the hotel, and thus saved us
from spending a night in the mountains, exposed to
the Liberals, who were only held in check by their
fear of the French.

A three hours' ride on the railroad brought us to
Vera Cruz, which is, in November, a very pleasant
place. The houses are generally two stories high,
and the roofs are flat and covered with a very hard
mortar, which turns water perfectly. If the streets
were bridged, one could walk almost all over the
city on the tops of the houses. Much work is done
on the house tops, and chickens and turkies are
raised as in a yard, and in November and the winter
months no place could be so pleasant for sleeping
as the housetop.

The porters in Vera Cruz are a remarkable set of
men. They wear felt hats, with enormous brims
that reach over their shoulders, and I have seen
them with three or four hats on at a time, so that
the brims made a soft padding on the shoulder,
which had to sustain the weight of four hundred
pounds. ▮▮▮▮▮lemen told me that he knew a por-
ter to ▮▮▮▮▮▮▮ ▮ hardware, weighing between

seven and eight hundred pounds, and I have seen enough to make me believe it. They are more Spanish than Indian.

After I had been in Vera Cruz a few days, the agent at the depot told me that I would have to take away my baggage, as they were clearing out the warehouse, to make room for Maximilian's baggage, which was expected the next day. I then felt confident that he would soon leave Mexico, and I was very much surprised to learn that he had yielded to the entreaties of representatives of the priests and property-holders of Mexico, and returned to the capital.

While I was truly sorry to learn his subsequent fate, I was not at all surprised. I saw and heard enough to satisfy me that he was one of the most kind hearted rulers in the world, and that he had most fully identified himself with Mexico, and that according to his ability he labored for the good of Mexico. In Vera Cruz, Cordova and Orizaba, where his authority was supreme, we had better order, better laws, more certain justice and much lighter taxes than I have any hope of seeing again while I live.

I think that the want of political ability as a statesman was the one great want   imilian. Marshal Bazaine may have   but

Maximilian would not be advised by him. I think that the Empress Carlotta had the ability, but though she was the most accomplished princess of Europe, and even beloved by Maximilian's enemies, he would not take her advice.

Maximilian was exceedingly fond of horses, and I think that if he had loved them enough to confine himself to them, and to give *her* the reins of the *people*, while he held the reins of the *horses*, it would have been a wise distribution of power, and the very salvation of Mexico.

That the enemies of Maximilian were destitute of principle is evident from their opposing the claims of General Ortega, a white man and a gentleman of literary, military and legal merit, and the Chief Justice of Mexico, and, as such, the constitutional President of Mexico until a new election should be held. But they trampled on the Mexican constitution, and helped a blood-thirsty half-Indian to usurp the office constitutionally belonging to the honored and accomplished General Ortega.

The mines of Mexico are wonderful for silver and gold. Three thousand mines have been already discovered, but only one hundred and fifty are worked, and yet these produce about $20,000,000 a year.

A traveler in Mexico says that two poor Indian brothers lived in a little town in northern Mexico, on the borders of a stream, and that one of them tried to buy a quart of Indian corn one morning, but could not get credit for it. That night there was a great rain, and the banks of the stream were over-flowed, so that the surface of the earth opposite the town washed off. The next morning the brothers, looking across the swollen stream, saw some pieces of silver on the bank, and swam over and picked up a good deal, and laid claim, according to Mexican custom, to the mine thus discovered; and when they had silver and credit enough.

During that year the mine produced $280,000 and the poor Indians did not know what to do with it. They made very little change in their living, as to dwelling, clothing or eating, and really had no use for so much money; but one of them filled a bag with dollars on a feast day, and called the people together and scattered the dollars among the crowd. It was a very novel amusement and vastly entertaining to the people, who must have regarded the poor Indian as a most eloquent actor and entitled to hearty applause. The Indian himself was greatly delighted at the performance of the people, and re-peated his original performance on subsequent festivals.

It cannot reasonably be expected, that Mexico should flourish, while the Christian Sabbath is so little regarded. On Sunday morning, many of the people go to the cathedrals and churches, for a little while, but nearly all day the stores are open, and in the cities, the afternoons are devoted to chicken fights, bull fights, and gambling. Even the priests are gamblers. One of them frequently passed our door in Cordova, on Sunday at three o'clock, going to the bull fight, with a fighting chicken under his arm, and a bag of dollars in his hand.

And yet, it was understood that these same priests would impose severe penance on any who might be known to have read the Bible.

While we lived in Cordova, one Sunday a little before dinner, the son of our landlord stopped at our door, and seeing one of our daughters, reading in a New Testament, half English and half Spanish, asked her what book she was reading. She invited him into the room and handed him the book. After he was seated he opened the book at the fourteenth chapter of the Gospel of John, "Let not your heart be troubled," &c., and read the Spanish with the most intense interest. He was too much absorbed to notice anything around him for nearly an hour; when seeing him so deeply interested, as book he was reading, but he did not hear her, till she raised her voice and called out "Francisco, Francisco," when he looked towards her, and answered. She asked him "What book are you reading?" He said. "It is most beautiful." "What is it?" she asked. He then turned to the title page, and read the name, when she immediately said, "You ought not to read that book, for if the priest should hear of it, he would impose very heavy penance on you." He replied, "I did not know it was wrong to read this book, and you never told me it was wrong."

Now, here was a youth of about twenty, who was charmed with the first chapter he had ever read in the New Testament, while many in our own country seem scarcely to value our great privileges.

On a trip I once made, I had an Indian driving the wagon, and I took out my Testament and read the twenty-fifth chapter of Matthew to him, in Spanish, and at its close, he said it wes "beautiful, *very* beautiful." I then talked to him in Spanish, and asked him how the Mexicans felt when they died. He said they were very sad, but bore it as well as they could. I asked him if he ever knew a Mexican to die happy, and he said he never heard of such a thing. I told him that, in my country, it was often the case and ... e that the dying person was exceedingly happy ... ll

others in the room were weeping. He was amazed
at it, and could not understand how it could be. I
asked him if he was sure that he loved God with
all his heart, and was sure that God loved him as
his child, would he be sorry to go to live with God,
if God should call him. He said, "No." I said, if
you do not know that God loves you, and feel that
you love him with all your heart, you will be afraid
to die. But my people, when they felt that they
were sinners, and that God was angry with them,
prayed till they felt that the Holy Spirit had come
into their hearts, to fill them with joy, and make
then *know* that God had pardoned all their sins, for
the sake of our Lord Jesus Christ, and then they
loved God, so that they were not afraid to do their
duty, and were not afraid to die.

Miguel was astonished at all this; and this talk
increased my desire to be useful to the Spanish race,
which has sent so many martyrs to the Kingdom of
Heaven. I had hoped to preach, in Spanish, to tens
of thousands of the Mexicans, and to see thousands
of them converted, and to hear hundreds of happy
converts shouting, in old fashioned Methodist style,
the highest praises of our glorious Redeemer; but
these joys are not for me but for some others, who
shall bring glad tidings of the Gospel to the
people of God.

, The religion of the Bible has never prevailed in Mexico, and I cannot think that this country, so rich in minerals, so delightful in climate, so grand in scenery, with its rich table lands, so elevated and healthy, will much longer suffer a "famine of hearing the words of the Lord."

Old Spain, as well as New Spain, can now re ceive the Gospel freely, and in both countries the Bible circulates without authorized opposition; and the lands where the Bible and its readers were burned for heresy are now receiving the morning rays of the Sun of Righteousness. And who knows, but in the coming reign of the Messiah, in Mexico, as it was in Jerusalem, "a great company of the priests may be obediant to the faith."

The first steamer that left Vera Cruz for New Orleans, after our arrival, charged more than we could possibly raise, and when a New Orleans steamer unexpectedly came to Vera Cruz, with freight, we were unable to procure passage in her, without pledging our baggage for our fare. At last, the matter was arranged, and we took passage in the Alliance, and after a stormy voyage, we entered the Mississippi just as a furious norther set in, and darkened the heavens over the C▓▓▓. As soon as we reached New Orleans, I wen▓ ▓▓▓▓ ▓ce or the New Orleans *Christian Advocate.* ▓ I learned that the Louisiana Conference would meet in Baton Rouge in about a week, and I determined to try to get there.

I then called on a commission house, to which I had a letter from General Hindman, but the gentleman was absent from the city, and I could get no help towards getting my baggage released. I then asked a very accommodating clerk in the house if there were any Virginia merchants in the city, and I asked to be directed to them if he knew any. He kindly went with me to several whose relations I knew, and also to others whom I knew nothing of; and they kindly loaned me about two hundred dollars, and I immediately settled with the captain, and we went on board a river boat, on our way to Baton Rouge. We had a very pleasant trip, and found a very good home, and experienced great kindness from our people and preachers during the Conference.

Bishop Payne presided, and very kindly introduced me to the Conference, as one whom he had known for about twenty years. I stated my case to the Conference, and asked to have a circuit assigned me, as I wished, above all things, to be engaged in the Methodist Min——

I w—— the Delhi circuit, which had not h—— having been ruined by the war, and repeated overflows of the Mississippi. Our traveling expenses from Baton Rouge came to $70, and after spending a month on the circuit, and preaching around at the principal appointments, the brethren made an effort to raise something for my necessities; and after trying out of the church, as well as among the members, they only raised $25.36, less than half the traveling expenses, for which one of the brethren had bound himself.

I saw that I could not live there. What should I do? I thought that I might make something by lecturing on Mexico, up in Missouri, or other places, beginning at Memphis; and I started out, hoping to make enough during the winter to support me on the circuit the rest of the year. When I got to Memphis, I found that no interest was felt in Mexico, and the expenses, such as room-rent, lights, fuel, taxes, &c., would probably be more than the receipts.

I then thought I would continue my trip, preaching and soliciting help for my circuit as a missionary field, as it really was: and leaving some kind friends in Memphis, I did myself the great pleasure of calling on my venerable friend, and first presiding elder, Rev. Moses Brock, who gave me my license to preach forty-four years ago This was a memorable visit. I never can forget it. But this

most remarkable man has, since my visit, been
taken to his reward, and it is with the warmest
emotion that I hope to meet him, with the rest of
the heroes of the Gospel warfare, in the weary
pilgrim's home.

In Jackson, Tenn., I met an old friend, Rev.
Amos W. Jones, president of the Female College
at that place, and had some very happy meetings
with the brethren. They were very kind to me
there, as also at Brownsville, on the way to St.
Louis. The thermometer was below zero when I
reached that city, and I soon found my way to the
hospitable dwelling of my old friend, Rev. Dr. W.
A. Smith, where I was most kindly received by all
the family, who were surprised to find me so much
out of my latitude.

For several weeks I attended meetings at the
Centenary church, of which Dr. Smith was pastor,
and enjoyed the services very much. I was in a
happy frame of mind while in St. Louis. The re-
membrance of former happy times, and of recent
dangers and privations, and the considerations of
present want, and the glorious prospects of eternal
blessedness so wrought upon me, that it was one of
the happiest seasons of my life.

One night I was going to church through one of
the finest streets of the city, and saw on each side

brown stone mansions with marble steps and costly windows, and all the signs of wealth, while I was shivering with cold because of the threadbare raiment I wore; and I commenced repeating to myself:

" No foot of land do I possess,
No cottage in this wilderness,
A poor wayfaring man ;
I lodge awhile in tents below,
And gladly wander to and fro,
Till I my Canaan gain.

Nothing on earth I call my own.
A stranger to the world unknown,
I all their goods despise;
trample on their whole delight,
And seek a city out of sight,
A city in the skies.

There is my house and portion fair,
My treasure and my heart are there,
And my abiding home;
For me my elder brethren stay,
And angels beckon me away,
And Jesus bids me come.

I come, thy servant, Lord, replies,
I come to meet thee, in the skies,
And claim my heavenly rest;
Now, let the pilgrim's journey end,
Now, O my Saviour, brother, friend,
Receive me to thy breast."

My heart was so transported with joy at the contemplation of these heavenly views, that I envied not the owners of these fine houses, but felt that I would not give my interest in that "house not made with hands eternal in the heavens," for all the things of this earth.

I continued my trip up the river to Jefferson City and Glasgow, and preached in both places, and was very kindly received by the brethren. In Glasgow I found some of my old acquaintances, and felt more like I was in Old Virginia than anywhere else, and was very liberally assisted.

When I returned to St. Louis I found that I could not get enough to support me on my circuit, and I tried to get a circuit where I might make out the rest of the year, though it might be one thousand miles from my family; but I could find none. The brethren in St. Louis, and the other places named, have my heartfelt thanks for their kindness, and but for their goodness we must have suffered very much.

Having spent about a month in Missouri, I went down to New Orleans, and, at the suggestion of Dr. Keener, I went to the dedication of the new Methodist church in Houston, Texas, and on my return I was delayed by high water, so as to miss the boat to Delhi.

This gave me most unexpectedly a spare week in New Orleans; and as there was a great deal of excitement on the subject of emigration to Brazil

Venezuela, and British Honduras, I went around and made enquiries about all these places. Two persons offered to pay my fare to British Honduras, and one of them offered me great assistance, if I should like the country and determine to settle there. When I considered that in a few months the supplies I had received during my trips would be exhausted, and that the flat lands on the Mississippi were all under water, and that there was a very poor chance of support from a circuit now more like a lake than a cotton-field, I thought it was my duty to accept the offers of my friends, and make a trip to British Honduras to look at the country.

Accordingly, I went up to see my family, and found the country, with very few exceptions, navigable for large boats, and after a few days' preparation I started to the Mississippi in a little skiff made of plank, and after two days' paddling over the public road, which we could scarcely touch with our paddles, I reached the great river, a distance of forty miles, and took a boat for New Orleans.

After a few more days I started, in the steamer *Trade Wind*, for British Honduras, about nine hundred miles from New Orleans. About twenty emigrants were on board, and we had a pleasan'

trip of about six days, ending in the harbor of
Belize, the capital of the colony.

Belize is a pleasant town of about seven thousand
inhabitants, of whom about three hundred are English, Scotch, Americans and other white people, and
the rest are of African, Spanish and Indian races.
The African race is much the most numerous, and
nearly all the common laborers are of that class.

Some of the houses are very handsome, especially
the governor's house, which is built of mahogony,
and the Wesleyan chapel, which is built of brick
and Mahogany, with pine floors. This was built
mostly by funds sent from England for the use of
the Wesleyan missionaries, who have a flourishing
society and mission school, nearly all of the African
race. There are two churches served by ministers
of the Church of England, a Scotch Presbyterian
church, a Baptist church, and a Roman Catholic
church, all very well attended.

Sundays are more rigidly kept in Belize than in
any other town I ever knew. Nothing but *medi-
cine* is sold on Sunday. Even milk is not allowed
to be sold.

There are several very large wholesale stores, and
as the import duty is only about ten per cent., goods
are cheap, especially linen, woolen, and very light
summer goods. There is no license charged for

selling anything, except a license of $200 a year for selling intoxicating drinks. There is a revenue or excise tax of one cent a pound on sugar made and used in the colony, and a similar tax of forty-seven and-a half cents a gallon on all rum made and used in the colony.

These are all the taxes I ever heard of in Belize. Those who consider a national debt a blessing, and heavy taxes a luxury, would have great complaints against British Honduras.

The houses of Belize look odd for want of chimneys, as the weather is so warm that no fires are needed, except in the kitchens.

The markets are very well supplied with fish, turtles, lobsters, clams, conchs, &c., of good quality, and very cheap. The vegetables and fruits of the tropics are very plentiful, though much dearer than in Mexico, and the butchers' meats cannot be praised for quality nor price.

Soon after reaching Belize, I joined a party of Southerners, and made a trip up the Belize river, at the mouth of which Belize is situated, in a large boat, called a pitpan, with an awning or cover, sufficient to shelter six persons from the sun and rain.

The pitpan is dug out of a large tree, of mahogany or Spanish cedar, about forty-eight feet long, abou forty inches wide, and nearly flat on the bottom, and about eighteen inches deep in the middle, but getting more shallow toward each end, where the depth is only about four inches and the width about two feet. The timber is trimmed off the bottom to correspond to the depth of the boat, and thus for about four feet from each end it is out of the water.

This style of boat is the best for dragging over the shoals and for steering rapidly, so as to shun the rocks and trees, where the descent is rapid; for the steering is done with paddles at both ends, which is the only practicable way in a narrow and swift current, and especially a crooked one.

The first seven miles we had no banks, but swamps, and then low banks, liable to overflow, and only good for cocoanuts and mangoes, until we had gone twenty miles, when the banks became higher and good for pasturage.

For the next sixty miles the lands improved, till they became suitable for corn, sugar, and all tropical fruits. After getting about eighty miles above Belize, all the lands are very rich, and especially suited to sugar, and all tropical products of rich limestone soil, and on the hills and mountains coffee can be raised.

In all this region the pasturage is very superior, and any amount of cattle and hogs could be raised.

' About one hundred and forty miles above Belize the northern and southern branches unite, and about three miles above the fork, on the northern branch, is the place which I selected for my home.

All the lands in the region, until you go off from the rivers to the pine ridges, are exceedingly rich, and suited to sugar cane and coffee; the hills and mountains to sugar cane. These lands also are well suited to indigo, smoking tobacco, rice corn, and all tropical fruits and vegetables; and cotton grows very well, but the worms might destroy it.

Nearly all this country is covered with small mountains and valleys, and well supplied with good water by the rivers and creeks.

The low grounds, where vegetation is very luxuriant, are very much annoyed by mosquitoes and other flies, but if the space of twenty or thirty acres, on some high land or hill, is well cleared and kept free of everything except fruit trees and short grass, the wind will keep all such annoyances away, and make your home very pleasant.

From sunset to sunrise the climate is most delightful, and towards day cool enough for a blanket, and always cool enough for thin covering, and for a hearty appetite as soon as you get up in the morning.

42

From all I could see and hear, I was satisfied
that this region was very healthy, and it would be
a very pleasant home for me if we could have
enough society; and with this view I returned to
Belize, and made arrangements with Governor
Austin and other parties to furnish land on long
credit and at low rates to me and as many of my
countrymen as might settle about me.

By the next steamer I returned to New Orleans,
and wrote a piece for the New Orleans *Crescent*,
detailing the observations I had made and offering
to answer such questions as might be propounded
by persons feeling an interest in British Honduras.
I immediately wrote to my family to prepare to
come down to New Orleans, that we might go out
to Honduras as soon as we could make the necessary
arrangements.

The interest in Honduras became so great that it
was called the "Honduras fever," and "Honduras
on the brain." About two hundred letters were
written to me and duly answered, and many of the
writers said most positively that they would go to
Honduras as soon as they could sell their cotton and
wind up their affairs, and several asked me to select
their places near my own. Under these circumstances, I fully expected to have plenty of neighbors
for the support of a school and for religious and

43

social privileges, and by the terms of my contract
with the proprietors of the land I should have been
remunerated for all the land I should have settled
up for them, but not at the expense of my countrymen.

When my family arrived in New Orleans, I was
negotiating for passage on a sailing vessel, as being
much cheaper than the fare on the steamer, and we
were detained two weeks, during which we enjoyed
the hospitality of a kind friend. The first vessel I
had engaged disappointed us, after taking some of
our freight on board; and it was well for us, as she
had a terrible trip of it.

The next one was a very small schooner, of only
24¾ tons, and after we had put our freight and baggage on board, and she was ready to sail, the custom
house officers prohibited the captain from carrying
passengers, as the vessel was too small. But we had
already put our things on board, and paid a part of
the fare. After some consultation, the captain told
me to take my family ten miles down the river, and
have a light on the bank, till he should drop down
the river and take us on, about nine o'clock at
night.

According to this arrangement, we left New
Orleans in an omnibus, at about four o'clock, on
our way to British Honduras, and stopped on the

bank of the river, and at dark made a light and
waited for the schooner. About nine o'clock we
saw her coming, and soon she came to the shore
with a pretty hard thump, which, however, did no
harm to the schooner, but stirred up a mighty
quarrel between the captain and the owner — the
latter having given the order which produced the
confusion. The owner had hired the captain, and
had come only as a common sailor, and had no right
to give an order. Both were drinky, and the quarrel soon came to blows, and the powerful fist of the
owner soon bruised the eyes of the captain and
knocked out one of his teeth, which he never could
find.

The captain then took the vessel's papers and
jumped on shore, swearing that he would return to
New Orleans that night. The owner then cooled
down, and begged the captain to go on to Honduras,
but he vowed that he would not, and soon he was
lost in the darkness. We wondered how this matter
would end, and the cook and some others went to
look for the captain, but having failed to find him,
we returned to the schooner and fought mosquitoes
till day, when the captain appeared and told the
owner that on our account he would go on. The
owner made many acknowledgments and promises of
good behaviour, and we started along down the river.

The captain still feared that we might be stopped
at the forts at the mouth of the river, and taken
back to New Orleans. But we passed out into the
Gulf safely, but passed into the midst of a great
storm, which treated our little schooner as a mere
plaything — like a cork upon the waters. It was a
serious time, and our vessel was in bad trim, having
a deck load of plank, piled up so high as to be very
much in the way. The captain said this plank
must be thrown overboard, and the beautiful floor-
ing plank was soon floating in the Gulf, till there
was a string of it a mile long, I suppose.

But the storm still continued, the waves pouring
down the hatches, at times—for we could not keep
them closed all the time, and the pumps going. My
wife, though she had been a great deal at sea, and
once had been for fifty days out of sight of land,
said she thought we would never see land again.

But we were all calm, and I expressed the hope
that our prayers would be answered, and that we
should escape this danger. I felt no fear myself,
except for my family. I enjoyed the presence of
my Saviour, and felt that heaven is as near the
Gulf of Mexico as any other place. The noise of
the roaring winds, and the plashing of the waves,
would have drowned the words of prayer, if we
could have assembled in one place. So we had to

pray in our hearts, and hold on to anything suitable to keep from rolling about.

After about two days, the storm subsided; and now we had another trouble. There was no quadrant, sextant, nor chronometer on board, and how could we navigate, with nothing but the compass? None on board but myself had ever-been to Belize, and seen the headlands on the way, and the captain thought the only safe chance was to guess at the direction of Cuba, whose western headlands several of us had seen, and to keep far enough north to avoid getting on shoals in the night, and when we could see the mountains of Cuba, to steer south, keeping the island to the east of us.

When the day dawned, the mountains were in full view, and we steered south, about six miles from the land, till to our astonishment we found that we were sailing over rocks, not four feet from our keel. And the knowledge that the owner of the vessel was a desperate *pirate* (and probably another one on board also), did not increase the comfort of our reflections.

But our captain immediately took the helm, and bore off from the land; and after about half an hour we were relieved of the painful sight of rocks near the keel of our vessel.

About nine o'clock at night, we passed the light of Cape San Antonio, and knew we were in the Carribean Sea. The sea ran high, but the wind was steady, and sometimes for an hour at a time all hands went to sleep, having fastened the til'er with a rope; and thus our little vessel navigated herself. The current from the Carribean Sea into the Gulf of Mexico is always strong, and sometimes more so than at others, according to the strength of the trade winds. We found it very strong, and made but little headway against it; but after a voyage of eleven days, we started to go through the Keys into Belize, without a pilot, and got aground on some soft mud; but as our vessel was so small, we pushed off with poles, and soon came up with some fishermen, who were nearly done fishing, and for a bucket of ship biscuit took us into the harbor.

The next day I rented a house and moved into it, and commenced fixing up a little steamboat, with the assistance of the governor and merchants of Belize, and some of our countrymen; but not having the means necessary to make it a success, though I took it nearly one hundred miles up the river twice, it did not answer the purpose, and I took my family up to the place I had chosen in a pitpan, with a cover.

The current was so strong that it took us twelve days to make the trip, and we had rain every day but one.

We found plenty of houses, such as they were, at our new home: it having been settled by an enterprising Spaniard, who traded with the Indians, and made rum, until his conduct excited the suspicions of the government; and he then fled to Guatemala, where he was detected in a conspiracy to rob and murder, and, to prevent being executed, hung himself.

The houses, like all others in that wilderness-country, are made of posts, or forks, supporting a frame of poles, well tied together with vines (found abundantly in the woods), and covered with a very thick roof of bay leaves (like the palmetto leaves, but a great deal larger and affording perfect protection against the sun and rain). The walls are made of poles, two or three inches in diameter, tied to horizontal poles, which are tied to the posts, and the spaces of about three-fourth of an inch left between the poles for the tie-vines, give light enough, without windows. The floors are of good solid earth, and suit very well for fire, in rainy weather, wherever you choose to make it.

But floors of this sort afford a nursery and dwelling place for countless numbers of fleas, as we found to our great annoyance. Neither cold nor hot water would destroy them, nor anything else we tried; but after we had had four sheep staying in the house, every night for a week, we found that these nimble insects had more than their match, when they got tangled in the greasy wool; and our regard for sheep has greatly increased. Those who have dogs and hogs in warm climates, ought to have sheep, as an antidote for fleas.

· Another singular insect annoyance, in Honduras as well as Mexico, is the negua, which is very much like a small flea. It burrows under the toe-nails and finger nails, causing great itching; and in about twenty-four hours a little sack is formed, full of eggs, and if then picked out with a needle the itching soon ceases and the little sore is soon cured; but if neglected for several days, it makes a very disagreeable sore, especially in young children, who are very restless while you are picking out the sack; and little children are more troubled than grown people, because their feet are more tender and generally more exposed.

Another annoyance is the beef worm, which comes from an egg deposited in the flesh by a kind of fly, and which sometimes grows to be nearly an inch long, and is much larger at the bottom than at the top. The remedy is to put some fig juice or other mucilage, on a small piece of leaf tobacco, and stick it on the place for some half hour, to deaden the worm, and then squeeze till the worm pops out. It is very hard to squeeze it out otherwise, and if it is allowed to grow large it is very painful.

Another annoyance is the army ant. These little insects are not like the fire ants, stinging like fire, but formidable for their prodigious numbers. They seem to have engineers among them, who lay off the track for their march generally about twenty feet wide, and within which they keep. Their numbers are such that they completely cover the ground and everything else in their track. They will pass through one room and frequently there will be none in the other room, nor in the other corner of the same room. They go up on everything on their track, all over the top of the house, and among the leaves that cover it, and then the sound is exactly like the sound of snow falling on leaves; and every lizard and other living thing in the roof hurries away. They go down into every rat hole and snake hole, and every snake and rat and mouse that is old enough to escape dashes off. The very young ones are stung to death. And the natives say, therefore the snakes are so scarce.

In about four hours the whole army has passed by, and done no harm, but has been a great "terror to the evil doers" that live in holes; and has set an example of *honesty* that is not often followed by so called Christian armies.

There is another kind of ant, very large and numerous, that live on leaves, and have large cities under ground, the excavations from which are piled up into a large mound overhead, about four feet high and twenty feet across. The tracks to and from the mound are about four inches wide, and beaten down hard and smooth; and in the tracks near the mound the ant eater (something like the raccoon) makes a hole, and, as the ants tumble in, helps himself with great apparent relish.

The spotted tiger and the brown tiger are seen in the country, and frequently kill oxen and hogs, but very rarely attack men. Foxes sometimes, and opossums frequently, destroy fowls, if they are not properly secured. Alligators are found in all the rivers, but rarely do any harm.

Game is very abundant. Deer, antelopes, wild hogs, and various other quadrupeds, are frequently shot by good hunters. There is a very large bird, called currasow, about the size of a turkey, that is equal to the turkey in flavor and far more beautiful, and when domesticated is very tame, and is at the head of the feathered tribe. I had a beautiful pair of them, that I brought as far as New Orleans, but I was afraid I would lose them if I attempted to bring them to Virginia in the winter.

There are also wild turkeys, and some other large birds; and parrots in flocks of one hundred or more; maccaws, or parrot hawks, as some call them, mostly red, but partly blue, and under the body yellow, and all three colors of the very brightest hue. Their tails are about two feet long, and they are the most brilliant birds I ever saw, but their voices are as harsh as their plumage is showy. They are taught to speak like parrots, but are not as safely handled.

The most remarkable animal I saw in Honduras is the tapir, or mountain cow. It is about as much like a hog as a cow, and weighs, generally, about four hundred pounds, and the meat is very good. It spends a good deal of time in the water, with only its head sticking out. It has a very tough skin, and makes it way through thorny bamboo thickets without regarding them, and goes down the steepest banks of the river. Its upper lip, like the proboscis of the elephant, can be extended so as to take hold of a tree, or a dog; and the hoofs of its forefeet are very formidable when it is protecting its calf. If it finds a camp fire in the woods, they say it will scatter it with its forefeet and put it out, while all the rest of the animals are afraid of fire.

We frequently heard the cries of baboons near our house, though I did not often see them. I saw one that the natives had killed to eat, and they said it was very good; but it looked too much like a child for my use.

But I never refused to eat the iguana, a very large kind of lizard, living entirely on leaves, especially sweet potato leaves, and about four feet long. One is equal to a hen in quantity and quality.

Soon after reaching our homes we employed some Indians to clear away the bushes around the house, and to cut down the woods for a cornfield, and to fix up our houses, as several had requested me to do, and I went down to Belize to meet those whom I expected. But I found none of them. And this I did four times, when I heard that soon after I left New Orleans the army worm had been more destructive than ever before, and that some large fields did not produce a single bale of cotton.

I planted a crop of corn, and a very large crop of plantains and bananas, so that we should not fail to have enough to supply all who might come. But those who had lost their cotton could not come, and no family ever came but that of my son-in-law.

He got a job of surveying, and divided his wages
with us, and instead of sending the money he
bought us, in Belize, soap, cotton cloth, powder and
shot, and such other things as the Indians needed;
and I took some of the youngest children with me
and went to the Indian towns and sold these thing,
and traded for hogs, fowls, and other things.

One of these towns, where there were as many
Africans as Indians, was about four miles off, and
contained about forty houses; the next was eight
miles, with about seventy houses; the next, ten
miles, with about thirty houses; and the last on
that side of us, two miles further, with about twenty
houses. These last three were almost entirely
Indians, speaking the Maya language, the principal
language of Central America, and very few among
them could speak Spanish. On the other side of
us, near the border of Yucatan, was another town,
twenty-four miles off, of about eighty houses.

When ready for a trip, I would take one or two
of the children, each of us carrying a part of the
goods in a bag made of twine, like a seine, and
fastened to a band two inches wide, which came
over the shoulders and was supported by the fore-
head, so that the weight rested on the back, and
the bearer walked something like the Grecian bend
of the ladies. We took with us a pair of blankets,

and some coffee and provisions, and some matches
in a quinine bottle, that they should not get wet,
and some shavings of fat pine, to start a fire
quickly.

When night overtook us near some watercourse,
we used whatever shelters we found convenient, or
did without, according to circumstances; and after
cooking and eating our supper and kneeling in
family prayers together, and mending the fire, we
swung our hammock to trees, or lay down on the
blanket, and slept till about day, when we commenced our preparation for the day's journey,
taking only a little coffee and a little piece of bread
or sweet potato, until our regular hour of breakfast,
which was nine o'clock.

Having sold what we could, and traded for some
hogs and fowls, we would start late in the afternoon,
so as not to drive the hogs more than two or three
miles before night, that they might not be too much
fatigued. We drove the hogs by tying one hind
foot, and using a long switch very gently. At first
it was very hard to get them started out of town
and we had to drag them around several times, but
after we got started they did better, and the next
morning we generally had but little trouble, unless
we came to logs in the path too large for them to
jump over. When they came to a fork in the

narrow path in the woods, we kept the rope tight,
and as soon as we saw any disposition in the hog to
take the wrong path we held him till he turned
his head towards the proper route, and then the
rope was slacked and he went ahead right.

It was a very troublesome business at first, but
we soon became trained to it, and learned it very
well. The old hogs sometimes fought, and it was
dangerous to drive them. I took charge of such
myself, and as I always carried with me (as all the
men in the country do) a stout knife, or sword,
about thirty inches long, called a machete, I was
prepared to defend myself.

The mode of scalding the hogs so as to get off
their hair, was to wet one side with water, and
holding a blazing bay leaf over the wet hair till it
would slip easily, to scrape clean with knives, and
then to turn the hog over and scrape the other side
in the same way. I then assisted the children to
hang the hog up, and they preferred to do all the
rest. I did not like the sight of flowing blood, and
the children only asked me to hold the hog till one
could stick him, and then they claimed the right to
do all the rest, except the hanging up. The bones
were all cut out, and the rest of the meat could
then be preserved by salt and smoke, however warm
the weather.

When we brought fowls, they were brought in two-story baskets, on our backs. The loads we carried were generally about one-third of our respective weights, but I have carried more than half my weight—about twenty-five fowls, the most of them grown hens.

Fowls are frequently carried in rolls,.each fowl rolled up in a large leaf, and tied like a roll of paper. .I once saw five turkeys, rolled up and fastened to an upright board about ten inches wide, heads reversed, carried on a man's back. I wished then that I was a painter for a while, that I might sketch off that turkey show.

In those trips we were frequently caught in the rain ; and one night especially, we were without shelter and it rained for hours, but still the children slept soundly. As soon as light appeared, we started for home with the hogs, and felt no injury from our drenching.

The Indians are a very inoffensive race. They have no organization, except that in each town they elect an officer called the *alvalde*, who dispenses justice and checks disorder. Generally they are very honest. I have known a dozen of them to spend the night where we had a whole washing of clothes hanging up, and they did not take a single piece ; and indeed I never knew an Indian to stea

ıny clothes. Even in the town of Belize, we left
:lothes hanging all night out of doors, exposed to
:he street (for we had no enclosure around the
yard), and nothing was ever stolen. They are a
small and weak race of people, but do as much for
the money paid them as the generality of laborers.
They receive twenty-five cents a day and rations,
or $5 a month and rations, which consists of about
half pound of pork and seven plantains, or an
equivalent of corn, a day; while the Africans, or
Creoles as they are called, get $8 or $9 a month,
and require flour for a part of their rations.

ıThe Indians are very expert in the use of the
machete, which they use for cutting grass and
bushes, and even small trees, using the axe only for
large trees. They dig post-holes for building houses
with the *machete*, and I saw two of them dig a
grave with *machetes*, using turtle shells to throw
out the earth. They use no plow, nor hoe, nor
spade, in working or planting their crops. Corn
land is prepared by cutting down the bushes and
trees in the winter, and just before the rainy season
sets in, about June 1st. Fires are kindled about
noon, when the dew is all off, and the wind quite
nigh, over this patch of leaves and bushes, and in a
few minutes the flames reach to the tops of the
surrounding trees; and the bursting of the sap from

the thick stems sounds like the discharges of small
arms in battle, and can be heard for miles.

When the burning is over and the coals are ex-
tinguished, but little is left, except the stumps and
the large logs; and the Indian swings a little bag
of feed-corn at hic side, and takes a convenient
pole, trimmed like a chisel, and throws it into the
ground like a javelin, and then stands it up and
drops four or five grains of corn under its heel, and
draws it out. If the earth falls on the corn, and
covers it sufficiently, no more is done; but if necessary the corn is covered up with the foot.

The rows of corn are about five feet apart, and
we would consider that it was planted too thick;
but they prefer to have it thick, some say, to prevent
suckers from shooting up. The corn grows very
fast, and if the bushes were chopped down, when
it is a month old, it would be an advantage; but it
is rarely done, and generally there is no cultivation
whatever, and yet there is a heavy crop made.
When the corn is nearly three months old, it is
customary to bend down every stalk, just below the
ears, to prevent the corn from falling down in the
wind and rain, as well as to make it more difficult
for the raccoons to get at it. As soon as it is hard
the Indians carry it home on their backs, and use
what they need for themselves, and feed the rest to

their hogs and fowls, which are the only things that bring them money.

After the first crop is taken from the land, it is much more difficult to clean it up for another year's crop than it is to clear the same quantity of land by burning, and a new cornfield is made the next year, and the same field is not used again until there is enough vegetation on it to make a good burning. Yams, sweet potatoes, cymblins, and pumpkins, are planted in the cornfield, and yield abundantly.

The cahoon palm is a great tree. Its leaves sometimes reach the enormous length of forty-five or fifty feet, and are nearly ten feet wide, and one of them is nearly as much as a man can lift. The stems are larger than a man's leg, and are used for making fences to keep out oxen, as well as for walling-in houses. The tree bears annually about three bunches of nuts, nearly a barrel on each bush, and the nuts are about the size of a hen's egg, and requiring an axe to grind them. The kernel is about one inch and a half in length, of an oval shape, and tastes almost exactly like cocoanut, only it is tougher and drier. It makes a very fine oil nearly equal to olive oil.

The India rubber tree is very beautiful; with large, round leaves. When the bark is cut, the juice spurts out as white as milk, but soon turns black. It is collected from the tree while standing, but frequently the tree is cut down, and all the juice is collected in a few days, from the different cuts made along the body. The juice is then poured into a trough, and a strong solution of alum mixed with it, to curdle it, and the next day it is poured. on boards, slightly inclined, that the whey may run off. The curd is then beaten, and trampled, and formed into large cakes, and dried on a scaffold for several days, until quite hard, when it is ready for market.

There is not much of it in the region where I was, but it is found in great abundance farther south, on the coast of the Spanish Honduras, and still farther south to the river Amazon. The trade in India rubber turns out as much money, and as much sickness and death, as any trade I have heard of.

The mahogany business was formerly very extensive on the Belize river; but nearly all the works there have been abandoned, as also to a great extent in other parts of the colony, and sugar-making is taking the place of it. There are several reasons for this: It is much more expensive to get the remaining mahogany, which is distant from the rivers, than it was to get that which was near the water; and there are places in Mexico and Spanish Honduras where it is much more accessible than in British Honduras; and then the price of it is much less than formerly.

Cabinet-makers have substituted other kinds of wood in its place to a great extent; and the British government, which formerly used it very extensively for boarding up its ships of war, because it does not splinter as other kinds of wood and kill men when balls are shot through it, has a great deal of it on hand, and has no use for it in iron ships, which are now the fashion.

It was a great business once, and employed a very great capital, and thousands of laborers. At all suitable places on the rivers, where the banks were high, houses were built, a large ox pen was constructed, and all around the houses a large clearing was made for pasturage. Wide, good roads were made, and very powerful trucks, with solid wooden wheels, about two and a half feet in diameter and nearly a foot thick, were furnished with seven pairs of large oxen to each truck.

Large quantities of fat pine wood were collected for torches, as it was too hot for the oxen to haul in the heat of the day. The hunters found the trees, and the cutters opened the way for the trucks; the trees were cut down and squared, some of them

four or five feet square; and, as suon as the dry
weather had hardened the roads, all was excite
ment. The grass cutters, two to each team, climbed
the bread-nut trees, and broke off the twigs, full of
very thick mucilaginous leaves, and sometimes
gathered one hundred and fifty bundles of this
superior fodder from a single tree, and brought
them generally in boats up or down the river. The
oxen devoured their fodder, which is sufficient to
keep horses or oxen fat while at work without anything else. The oxen, preceded by the torch-
bearers, hauled the great timbers to the bank, to be
tumbled into the river for passage to Belize by the
next flood. The experienced captains and their
associates kept everything busy among the seventy
men who composed the gang, until the first heavy
rain wound up the hauling business for the year by
turning the roads into mud.

Each log was branded, and when the flood carried
them down the river they were caught by an enormous chain stretched across the river, twenty miles
above Belize, which is about the head of tide water,
and when they were let through this boom, as it is
called, they were rafted together, and floated down
to Belize, where they were drawn up on the yards
and nicely hewn over, and then floated to the ship
and stored in the hold, all the vacant places being

filled up with cocoanuts in the husk. Very large profits were formerly made by this trade, but very little is made now.

Logwood and fustic, for dyeing purposes, are also exported, and I think a factory for preparing extract of logwood would be one of the most profitable investments that could be made in the colony.

Cocoanuts are raised on the sandy beaches, all along the coast, and about two hundred nuts are obtained annually from each tree. You see them of all sizes on the trees at the same time, from the bloom to the full grown nut, and they fall when they are ripe. They are used for feeding hogs and fowls, and for making oil, as well as for eating.

As no settlers came to our neighborhood, and the surveying had ceased, our circumstances became very straitened, and we suffered much for want of such fare as was required, especially for want of flour and butcher's meat. We had not the means to buy a cow, and we had to live mostly on hog meat and corn bread, and the vegetables and fruits of the country. But we needed variety of food, and we could not have our health and strength, for want of suitable diet. We had chill and fevers, and frequently we had no quinine or other medicines. But I am satisfied that our sickness was owing much more to the diet and exposure and fatigue,

than to the climate, and that if we had had the
means and suitable society we should have been
healthy and happy, and in five years, when coffee
trees were bearing, we should have been very
prosperous.

But after having been two years in the wilderness, fifty miles from the nearest white family, with
no prospect of society, I began to think about trying
to return to Virginia. My brother had written to
me from Richmond, urging me to return, and
quoting some kind messages of my friends; and I
wrote to him that if I could get the means I should
like to return and enter the Conference, at its
session in Richmond, November 10th, 1869.

After writing this letter, I reviewed our life in
Honduras, with feelings of lively gratitude for the
deliverancies from danger, and especially for the
preservation of our little son, when he was lost and
spent the night in the thick forest, and again when
he was washed out of a boat in the river, by the
violence of the current, which washed the boat
under water, and under some limbs and logs that
held it out of sight, so firmly that about ten Indians
were required to get it out, and kept under till he
was nearly drowned. We had not as much as a
dollar to pay our way down to Belize, and the boat-
man charged us $15, but consented to take our old

chairs, tables, and some other things for our fare
I concluded to go to Belize, and trust to the Providence of God for our return to Virginia. When
we got to Belize, a kind gentleman loaned us the
use of a new house, which was very convenient;
and I sold a piece of India rubber belt and a few
fowls, and got a few dollars to keep house on.

But no letter had come from Richmond, because
the steamer *Trade-Wind* had been lost in the Gulf,
with all the mails, soon after leaving New Orleans;
and we had to wait about six weeks, till a new
steamer was put on the line; and on the 11th of
November I received a letter, in which a kind friend
authorized me to draw on him in Richmond for
$100, to pay my way to Richmond, while my family
could remain in Belize, two thousand miles off, till
I could get assistance to send for them. By return
steamer I came to New Orleans, and sent my family
a little money, but a kind merchant in Belize learn-
ing how little it was, gave them fifty dollars in
silver, which is the currency of the country. As
soon as I got to Wytheville, in Virginia, I found
the stationed preacher, whom I had baptized in his
infancy, thirty years ago, and spent a very pleasant
time with him and the brethren, and I preached at
night and received material aid very liberally.

In Lynchburg, Richmond, Petersburg, Norfolk, Portsmouth and Suffolk I met many old acquaintances and friends, who kindly helped me, so that I sent on the means to pay the fare of my family from Belize to New Orleans, where they kept house as economically as possible at a place I had provided for them.

But then it was necessary to provide for their living in New Orleans, and to procure their thick winter clothing, without which it would be dangerous to come to Virginia in the winter, after so long a residence in a hot climate; and the fare by steamer from New Orleans to Baltimore, the cheapest and most pleasant route, was another considerable item. I went to Baltimore to see about the matter, and there and in Alexandria received some help; and then I went to Mecklenburg, Virginia, among my old friends, to whom I preached in '38 and '39, and where, but for their poverty, I could have obtained all I needed in a few days.

The agent of the steamer in New Orleans was so kind as to wait for the fare till I should be able to send it; and my family, escorted by an American friend, came on the steamship *Cuba*, in February; and I met them in Baltimore and took them to Charlottesville, to the house of a friend, whose kindness has furnished more than half the expense of our return to Virginia; and may this friend, and the other who paid my passage, and all others who have helped us, be abundantly rewarded by the Father of mercies.

After nearly two weeks spent in the very pleasant family of our friend, we came to Petersburg, where we thought it best to live on account of the schools for the children and the cheapness of house rent. After a search of some days I found a suitable house and rented it; but we had no furniture, and only three dollars to start on. But the kindness of friends again appeared, for one loaned us a bed; and another, a bedstead; and another, another bed; and another, a bedstead; another, chairs; another, tables; another gave us a cooking stove; another a load of wood;—so we commenced housekeeping, and before the three dollars had quite gone, a friend whom I had not seen for thirty years came to see us, and gave me $5 in gold. Before my family arrived I had tried to get some ministerial work, and had made enquiries in four presiding elders' districts, but I could hear of none; and my friends Hummer and Laurens, general agents of the St. Louis Mutual Life Insurance Co., had given me work with them, and promised me some assistance in advance. Before I had used this last $5, this

help came; and I started on a trip to Gatesville,
Edenton, Elizabeth City and other places, where the
people were generally too hard run to insure their
lives, until the next crop shall come in. As soon
as I discovered this, I determined to operate as an
evangelist or missionary, preaching among my
friends as much as my circumstances will allow,
and depending upon their help, until I can find
some ministerial work that will be suitable to my
condition. When that will be I cannot now see.
I am in debt for advances I have received from
several friends,- for some house rent, and several
months' schooling of my children. I have no
furniture worth naming; our supply of clothing is
very limited, and what I wear is not worth giving
away, having done good service before it was given
to me. I have no horse, no watch, nor even the
means of moving our things to another part of the
town, much less to a circuit. But on the other
hand, we have reason to be thankful to our
Heavenly Father, that we _have had_ a full average
of the world's comforts, and no deaths, and but a
little sickness in my immediate family, for twenty
years; and considering the benefits of our observations and experiences in foreign lands, especially to
the children, we do not regret our course for the
last four years. I have never had a thought of

regret all this time. I have prayerfully tried to find out what was my duty. I preached wherever I could, in Belize as well as Mexico; I distributed tracts, where I could find men who could read them, and exhorted them to serve their God, and to meet me in Heaven, which some of them, with tears, promised me they would do.

The most pleasing employment I could have on earth, would be laboring on a circuit with twenty-four appointments in four weeks, as Mecklenburg circuit was in 1838, and seeing such times as we had that year.

In conclusion, I earnestly pray that the writer of this little book, and all its readers, may so live that we all may have "an abundant entrance administered unto us into the everlasting kingdom of our Lord and Saviour Jesus Christ. Amen."